CLANCY OF THE OVERFLOW

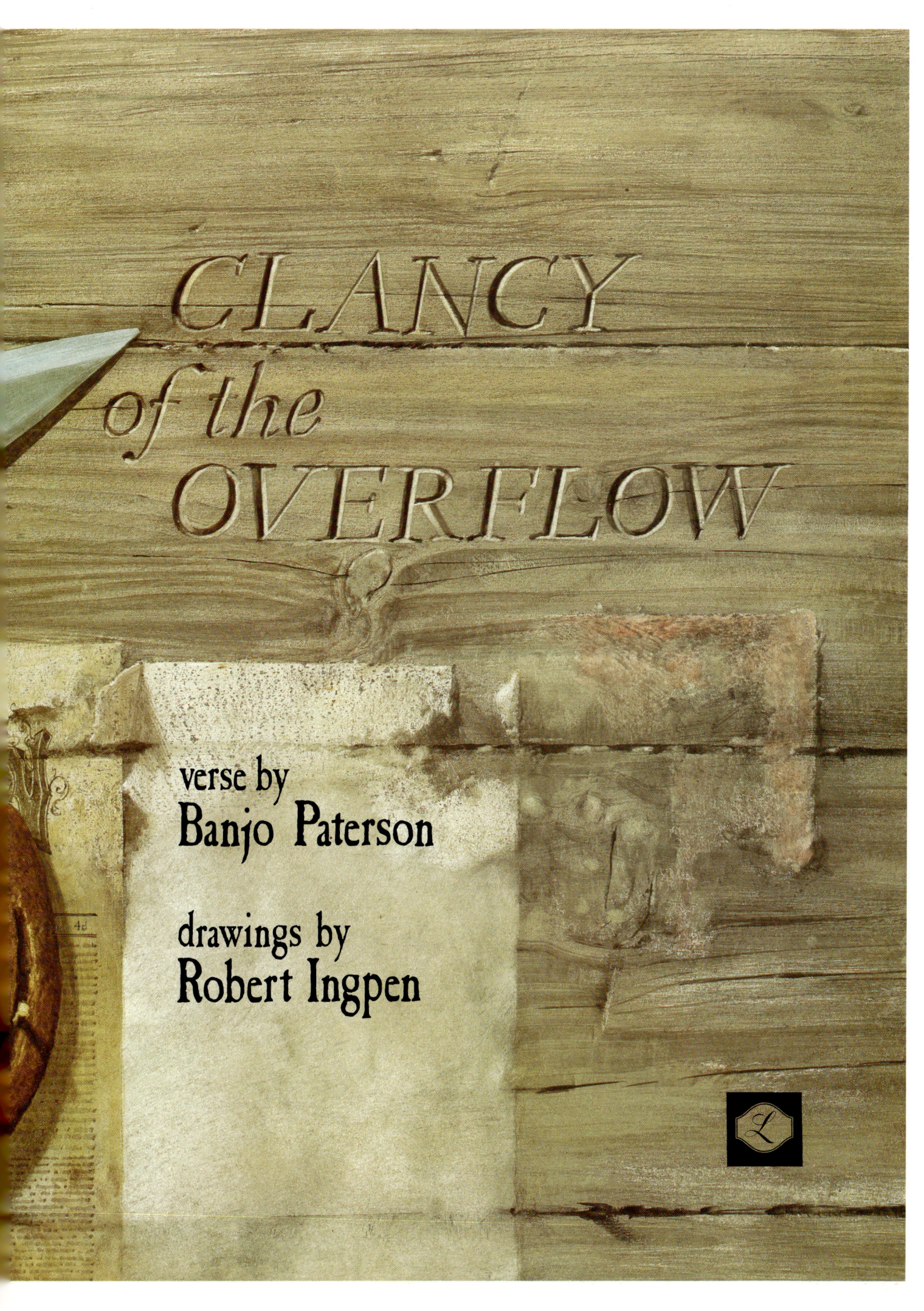

CLANCY of the OVERFLOW

verse by
Banjo Paterson

drawings by
Robert Ingpen

Books by Robert Ingpen

Marking Time: Australia's Abandoned Buildings
Pioneer Settlement in Australia
The Unchosen Land
The Voyage of the Poppykettle
Australian Gnomes
Pioneers of Wool
Australia's Heritage Watch
Australian Inventions and Innovations
Robe: A Portrait of the Past
Storm Boy (illustrations for de luxe edition. By Colin Thiele)
Lincoln's Place (by Colin Thiele)
River Murray Mary (with Colin Thiele)
Chadwick's Chimney (with Colin Thiele)
Paradise and Beyond (with Nick Evers)
The Night of the Muttonbirds (with Mary Small)
Turning Points in the Making of Australia (with Michael Page)
Aussie Battlers (with Michael Page)
The Runaway Punt (for children) (with Michael Page)
Lifetimes (with Bryan Mellonie)
The Great Bullocky Race (with Michael Page)
Click Go The Shears

Distributed by Sandstone Books
56 John St, Leichhardt NSW Australia 2040

Published by Lansdowne Publishing Pty Ltd
Level 1, The Argyle Centre
18 Argyle Street, The Rocks, NSW Australia 2000

First published by Rigby Publishers Adelaide 1982
Reprinted 1982
Reprinted by Lansdowne Publishing Pty Ltd (limp) 1997

Design © copyright Lansdowne Publishing Pty Ltd 1982
Illustrations © copyright R.R. Ingpen 1982
Colour seperations by Enticott-Polygraph, North Melbourne, Victoria
Printed by Everbest Printing Co. Ltd, Hong Kong

ISBN 1 86302 577 4

All rights reserved. Subject to the Copyright Act 1968,
no part of this publication may be reproduced, stored in
a retrieval system, or transmitted, in any form, or by any
means, electronic, mechanical, photocopying, recording or
otherwise, without the prior written permission of the publisher.

LOOKING FOR CLANCY

THE LEGENDS OF EVERY NATION reflect the 'inner lives' of their peoples, but Australia is perhaps unique in having two bodies of legends reflecting totally different cultures. Those of the Aborigines are of unknown origin, but those of the white Australians are, again, unique because we can trace them to their sources.

Like the legends of other countries, they show us to ourselves not necessarily as we are, but as we would like to be. The difference between our legends and those of other countries is that theirs usually involve supernatural folk heroes: King Arthur of Britain, Maui of Polynesia, Cuchulain of Ireland, Barbarossa of Germany, and so on. Such heroes reflect the special charisma which each race likes to believe is a unique quality.

But we Australians, more pragmatic and realistic, know there is nothing supernatural about our background. We prefer our heroes to be genuine personifications of what we would like to be. In a similar way to those of other countries they must reflect our 'inner lives,' but they must be dinkum Aussie battlers too.

The question is: What *would* we like to be? Our lifestyle shows that we prefer to be townsfolk. Seventy per cent of us are crammed into the eleven principal cities, and most of the rest of us live in other cities or towns. This trend has existed since goldrush days, and the average Australian has always preferred the comfort and security of communal living to the hardships and isolation of the bush.

Flowers for the Dead.

AN UP-COUNTRY SKETCH.

[I] HAD a most singular adventure last month. It came about in this way. I was stopping at Rose Hill one of the biggest stations on the Queensland Downs, with my friend Davis, the manager. Hamilton, the nearest township, is about 35 miles off, and, having business there, I got the loan of a horse from him, intending to ride over. I had never gone before, but the road seemed very simple. Rose Hill is a cattle-station in the middle of sandy but well-timbered country. It is quite wild; very little of it being fenced off, the cattle of one station was disquieting. And all the while hunger and thirst gnawed at stomach and mouth, and the miles to the belt of trees which surrounded the township seemed something more than interminable.

But all things end at last, and, as the lane suddenly broke into the line of trees, both horse and rider brightened up, and the stirring strains of "St. Patrick's Day in the Morning" were (rather inappropriately, it is true) whistled out cheerfully into the dark. Still six or seven miles to go, but already in front of me I could see lights — the lights of some house that was the outpost of kindly civilised men living in community together.

As I came closer I was struck by the number and brilliancy of those lights. Their position lent view. I was surprised; then a little startled, but held on, keeping my gaze fixed on her.

She was standing on the verandah — on the edge of the verandah. I was struck by her vague attitude. The light of the candle which she held fitfully illumined her face.

There was not much breeze out in the open plain. Here in the scrub there was little or none. The candle flickered and burned steadily, with a regular alternation. What was she about? She seemed heedless of everything. The sound of my horse's hoofs must now have been distinctly audible to her. I crossed the road and came along the fence, all the while keeping my gaze fixed on her.

She held the candle loosely, letting it hang forward. She was in her night-gown, a long nightgown that reached to her feet. Her hair, long and thick, was all about her neck and throat. Her head was sunk back, as it were, into her shoulders, which stooped forward and seemed marrow.

As I drew up at the gate, the candle steadied for a moment and I saw her face distinctly. The look of her eyes was enough. I concluded at once that she was either walking in her sleep or mad. I sat there and watched her.

She seemed irresolute, now turning a little backwards to her left, now making as if to advance. Her feet were moving uneasily, as if feeling their way forward. The verandah had one step, and it was a big one. Several times she felt out and down with her bare foot. Then her mind seemed to be made up. Down she came.

She was now in the path and almost six yards from me, directly facing [me]. It was a little [...] attention. She was [...] with her head thrust forward, [...] hurry I almost ran up against [...] a yard apart.

[...] embarrassed. Yet it was quite [...] not see me. Nevertheless I [...] looking aside at the candle on [...] guttering.

[...] her I stepped to it and took it [...] satisfied that there was no one, [...] peculiar movement, the shoul- [...] head sunk back into them, [...] by the door. I followed.

[...] passage opening by two [...] side rooms and running on [...] one of the back rooms. All [...] en, and light proceeded from [...] from that at the end of the [...] the door immediately on the [...] I followed.

[...] struck me was the fact that [...] number of candles lit in it. [...] everywhere. The next thing [...] stump bedstead, draped all in [...] running across the end of [...] Upon the bedstead, covered [...] was the corpse of an old

[...] standing between me and the [...] I had caught one glimpse of [...] Utterly bloodless, yellowy- [...] big and blue all over the [...] yes half covered with the [...] brown lips drawn back from [...] the figurement of incarnate [...] horrified, but irresistibly attracted. I neither advanced nor retreated. I stood still, candle in hand, and looked.

Then the girl began to speak. At first I could not, or did not, catch the words, but I felt they were a child's wail of pity over some unhappy person or thing.

"Oh, poor thing, poor thing, poor thing!" she said. "Oh, poor thing, poor thing, poor thing!" She lifted up her face and began to sing. It was one of the songs children learn to sing in chorus. She sang it absolutely as a child would, with just the same tone and regular marking of the time. I only remember two lines of it—
 "Buttercups and daisies,
 See the pretty flowers!"

And with that she began sorting out her flowers and leaves to put a nosegay of them on the pillow beside the ghastly face.

I drew closer, until I stood at the foot of the bedstead, and there I watched it all like a man in a miraculous dream.

She did not end talking and singing until she had strewn all the flowers about the face and shoulders of the dead body.

"Robin red-breast, robin red-breast," she said, "be sure to bury the dead people. The poor things, the poor things! Do not forget the poor people. Be kind to the dead people, be kind to the dead people! The poor things, the poor things!"

When she had done, she drew back and, saying several times "Good-bye, poor thing, good-bye!" slowly turned and went to the door. I gave one parting glance at the nose and teeth thrust up, through that confused shower of green and colour, geraniums, white verbenas, petunias, and a miscellaneous collection of leaves, and followed her down the passage and to the door of the second back-room, which was in the middle of the partition on the left, and was open, with light proceeding from it. She entered this.

I came to the door-way, putting the candle down on the table that was in the middle of the room, and looked in.

It was a bed-room with a large double bed in it. Two young girls lay in the inside of the bed, fast asleep. A candle was on the chest of drawers at

[...]

"Clancy of the Overflow."

[FOR THE BULLETIN.]

I had written him a letter which I had, for want
 of better
Knowledge, sent to where I met him down the
 Lachlan, years ago,
He was shearing when I knew him, so I sent the
 letter to him,
Just "on spec," addressed as follows, "Clancy,
 of 'The Overflow.'"

And an answer came directed in a writing unexpected,
(Which I think the same was written with a
 thumb-nail dipped in tar)
'Twas his shearing mate who wrote it, and verbatim
 I will quote it:
" Clancy's gone to Queensland droving, and we
 don't know where he are."

In my wild erratic fancy visions come to me of
 Clancy
Gone a-droving "down the Cooper" where the
 Western drovers go;
As the stock are slowly stringing, Clancy rides
 behind them singing,
For the drover's life has pleasures that the
 townsfolk never know.

And the bush hath friends to meet him and their
 kindly voices greet him
In the murmur of the breezes and the river on
 its bars,
And he sees the vision splendid of the sunlit plains
 extended,
And at night the wond'rous glory of the everlasting stars.

I am sitting in my dingy little office, where a
 stingy
Ray of sunlight struggles feebly down between
 the houses tall,
And the foetid air and gritty of the dusty, dirty
 city
Through the open window floating, spreads its
 foulness over all.

And in place of lowing cattle, I can hear the
 fiendish rattle
Of the tramways and the 'busses making hurry
 down the street,
And the language uninviting of the gutter children
 fighting,
Comes fitfully and faintly through the ceaseless
 tramp of feet.

And the hurrying people daunt me, and their
 pallid faces haunt me
As they shoulder one another in their rush and
 nervous haste,
With their eager eyes and greedy, and their stunted
 forms and weedy,
For townsfolk have no time to grow, they have
 no time to waste.

And I somehow rather fancy that I'd like to change
 with Clancy,
Like to take a turn at droving where the seasons
 come and go,
While he faced the round eternal of the cash-book
 and the journal—
But I doubt he'd suit the office, Clancy, of "The
 Overflow."

BANJO.

But in his 'inner life' he yearns nostalgically for a gallantry and gaiety which he believes to be his true birthright. He may in fact be a TV repairman or a solicitor's clerk, the descendant of generations of manual or clerical workers, and he knows he is locked into the city lifestyle, but his 'inner life' tells him he should be something entirely different.

By tradition, by song, story, and legend, an Australian should be a free and independent spirit galloping through the wide open spaces: vigorous, hearty, self-reliant, scornful of authority, exempt from the niggling problems and spiritual erosion of the cities. He should, in fact, be Clancy of the Overflow.

A. B. Paterson's ballad is an excellent example of the homegrown legends which we in Australia use as a substitute for the supernatural tales inherited by people of other lands. Like them, they both reflect and inspire our inner lives. Intentionally or otherwise, Paterson even structured the verses to show the deep schism between the outer and inner lives of Australians: the restrictions and realities of city life, and the nostalgic yearning for that wild freedom somewhere beyond the horizon.

The ballad may reflect a similar schism in the life of Andrew Barton Paterson. He was born, in 1864, as the son of a grazier, and he grew up in the bush until he was sent to school in Sydney. He lived during term-time with his grandmother, Mrs Robert Barton, who was a writer of published verse and a member of the literary circles of that period. In the holidays he returned to his father's grazing property.

This 'double life' must surely have had its later effect. Part of it was spent in the world of the intellect; the other part in the bush, in the heyday of the 'old' outback. It was a total swing from pen and ink to boots and saddles; from academic conversation to the downright opinions of drovers, stockmen, bullockies, and other bushmen, with their intricate knowledge of bush lore and legend. It was freedom, perhaps, after captivity.

Nevertheless he did well in captivity. He matriculated at sixteen, became a law student, and qualified as a solicitor. For the rest of his younger manhood, until he went to the South African War as a correspondent, he practised law in Sydney.

There, the two opposed aspects of his earlier life began to seek reconciliation and expression. Like his grandmother, he began to write stories and verses. Naturally they were coloured with his love for the bush and tinged with the wryly humorous, yarn-spinning characteristics of the old bush folk. In the fashion of those days he signed them with a nom-de-plume: The Banjo. This, the name of a station racehorse, was also a carryover from life in the open air.

His 'bush ballads,' published first in the 'Bushmen's Bible,' the old Sydney *Bulletin*, were popular because they appealed to both sides of the disparate Australian community. Bushmen recognised their ring of reality: city folk enjoyed their depiction of the free vigorous life beyond the settled areas. Everyone liked their racy freshness, good humour, and vivid imagery. The Banjo never wrote of bush life in the despondent, self-pitying Henry Lawson style, but always with the verve of young men trotting their horses out on a sparkling spring morning. He was sometimes accused of romanticising his subject but that was how it appeared to him.

In 1889, Paterson wrote the ballad which totally expressed the division in his own life and between city and outback Australians. It was 'Clancy of the Overflow,' published in the *Bulletin* in December 1889.

The ballad achieved immediate and lasting popularity. It struck a chord in the hearts of all those in 'dingy little offices;' those who, like Paterson, were daunted and haunted by the weedy, pallid-faced city crowds with their 'eager eyes and greedy.' Paterson seemed to have shown them the *real* Australian, in the roving free-spirited Clancy, and the *real* Australia in the 'vision splendid, of the sunlit plains extended.' These, and not the polluted city streets, were the longed-for birthright of Australians. Clancy, riding light-heartedly

singing behind the cattle, was what every true Australian would wish to be. Something seemed to have gone wrong, so that more and more Australians were trapped on the treadmill of commercialism, but reality never prevented anyone from dreaming.

Bush folk also acclaimed the ballad. They did not have to dream about the scenes and atmosphere which Paterson portrayed, because they experienced them every day, but they recognised him as a man who could encapsulate their experiences, in words with the swing and rhythm of sunlit days in the saddle.

The ballad has been almost continuously in print since 1889, and it has attracted so much analysis and discussion, whether around campfires or in the Aust. Lit. courses of universities, that it is sometimes difficult to remember it is not a folk legend but a set of verses written by a man who died only forty years ago. Clancy has become a folk hero, and many thousands of words have been written, and many barroom arguments hammered out, on whether he was a real person or not. The fact that so many people seem to need him to be a real person is further evidence that he is the Australian 'whom every man would wish to be.'

There were three Overflow Stations, in New South Wales and Queensland, and 'The Overflow' is sometimes used for the flood plains of the Macquarie. There was a well-known drover named Thomas Gerald Clancy, who died in 1914, and another named Thomas Michael Macnamara, whose relatives claimed that he was the original of Clancy and that his brother-in-law, Jim Troy, was 'The Man from Snowy River,' in which poem Clancy made a second appearance. It is also alleged that Paterson, as a solicitor, drew up T. G. Clancy's will.

There are other claims, rumours, and examples of wishful thinking. Paterson himself denied that Clancy, to his knowledge, ever existed. He said the ballad was inspired when he had to write, as a solicitor, to 'a gentleman in the bush who had not paid his debts.'

'. . . an answer came directed, in a writing unexpected (And I think the same was written with a thumbnail dipped in tar); 'Twas a shearing mate who wrote it, and *verbatim* I will quote it: "Clancy's gone to Queensland droving, and we don't know what he are."'

Probably the missing debtor was not named Clancy and no doubt Paterson's letter was not addressed 'just on spec' to The Overflow. But the incident, or something like it, would have been enough to set Paterson dreaming of escape to his beloved bush, far from the 'dirty, dusty city.' The balladist's imagination, seeking evocative words with swing and rhythm, would quickly have settled upon Clancy of the Overflow. Something like Smethers of Wonthaggi would certainly not have had the proper ring.

But the provenance of Clancy and the immortal ballad is really of no importance. Paterson's other famous ballads, 'Waltzing Matilda' and 'The Man from Snowy River,' have been subjected to just as much meaningless analysis. They have lives of their own, and they are forever woven into the tapestry of Australian lore and legend. Clancy is alive and well in the hearts and minds of Australians.

In this book, the artist has illustrated the ballad without wishing either to destroy or enhance the legend, but simply to say 'Here he is: how does he fit your mental picture of him?' We all have our own Clancy somewhere in our inner life.

Perhaps the best way to look for Clancy, in this collection of drawings, is to see behind the illustrations. They revolve around the ballad in a way that tries to capture the figure of Clancy as he might have been: the shearer, the stockman, the drover, and the focus of an Australian dream.

The first drawing (page 18) is either Clancy or one of his shearing mates. He was shearing in the Riverina in his twenties, and always with the blades. He and his mates wouldn't touch the newfangled mechanical shears. They said it was cheating, and all the art was gone.

In 1877 there was a boomer wool clip at The Overflow. Close on forty shearers, pickers, penners, woolclassers, rouseabouts (and the cook) worked for the moment captured in the drawing on pages 20–21. The last bales were being loaded on the wagon and the whole 'muster' including the boss and his family, gathered for the rum and the record. Can you pick Clancy there?

Sometime later he went droving. At times the stockyards were just a cloud of dust and you could barely see the steers. It was like the drawing on page 22.

A drover often broke his own horses, and the brumbies were all fire and go: as wild as hell in the makeshift yards. One kick in the shins and you were 'rats.' Clancy shared his passion for the open plains with his love to be close in with the mob and the smell and the contact . . . and the dust. This is shown in the drawing on pages 24–25.

At forty-three, Clancy may have looked like the drawing on page 26, although this is really only a study for the more detailed and colourful portrait on pages 32–33. The Banjo sits at his office desk, lit only by that 'stingy ray of sunlight.' Some might believe that Clancy is sitting in a pub, laughing at someone's bawdy joke.

On pages 28–29, he returns to the reality of endless saddle-hours in every type of weather, following the cattle as he 'rides behind them singing.' It is the time behind the excitement of the muster and the delivery at railhead.

On page 30 the drawing shows in detail his hat and drover's saddlebag, and the final picture is of Clancy at full gallop down a slope. This is the Clancy of Snowy River as well as of The Overflow.

The other drawings are of Sydney and its people in about 1900. They are based on the reality of city life at that time and show the place and its people very much as Paterson would have seen them.

There has been little real change in the ninety-odd years since

Paterson wrote 'Clancy.' City dress was more formal and less varied than today, and everyone wore a hat. Pollution derived from animal droppings, the dust of unsealed streets, primitive sanitation, and the garbage from street stalls and markets, rather than from the monstrous chemical effluvia which now shroud Sydney in whisky-coloured smog. But human nature never really changes. City folk still yearn for the freedom of the wide open spaces, while countryfolk still know the reality of isolation, hard heavy labour, and the climate which may bring drought, flood, or bushfire 'as the seasons come and go.'

Both sides have their own vision of Clancy. They cherish it in their inner lives, but when they seek its reality it becomes more and more evasive. Looking for Clancy is like looking for something we need urgently but have temporarily misplaced. The harder we look for it the more frustrated we become. Perhaps it is better to leave Clancy where he is: riding casually across the outback of the Australian consciousness, singing his song which echoes just beyond hearing, filling our dreams with all that we would like to be.

I had written him a letter which
   I had, for want of better
Knowledge, sent to where I met him
   down the Lachlan, years ago;
He was shearing when I knew him,
   so I sent the letter to him,
Just on spec, addressed as follows,
   'Clancy, of The Overflow.'

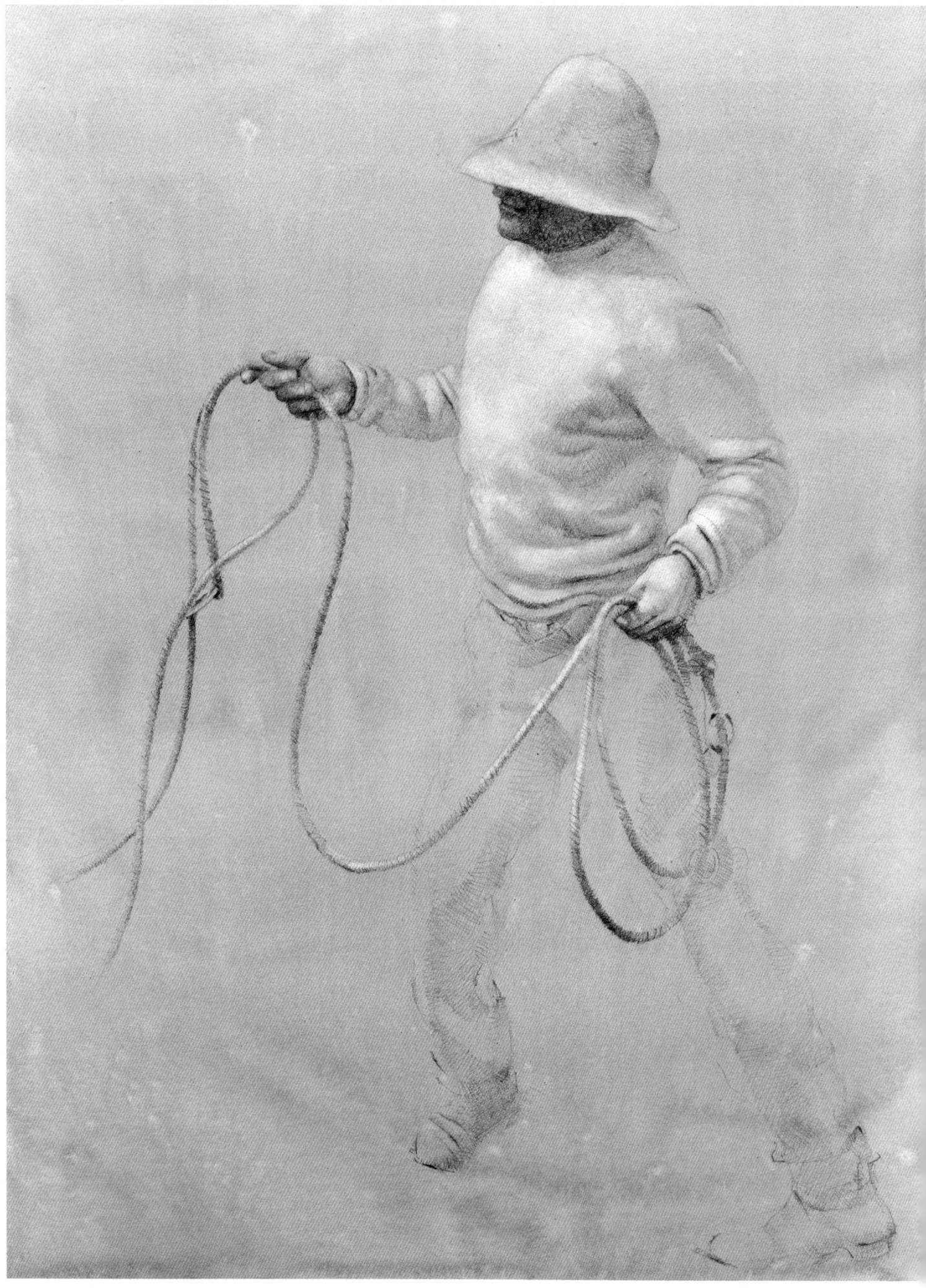

And an answer came directed
   in a writing unexpected
(And I think the same was written
   with a thumb-nail dipped in tar):
'Twas his shearing mate who wrote it,
   and *verbatim* I will quote it:
'Clancy's gone to Queensland droving,
   and we don't know where he are.'

In my wild erratic fancy
   visions come to me of Clancy
Gone a-droving 'down the Cooper'
   where the Western drovers go;
As the stock are slowly stringing,
   Clancy rides behind them singing,
For the drover's life has pleasures
   that the townsfolk never know.

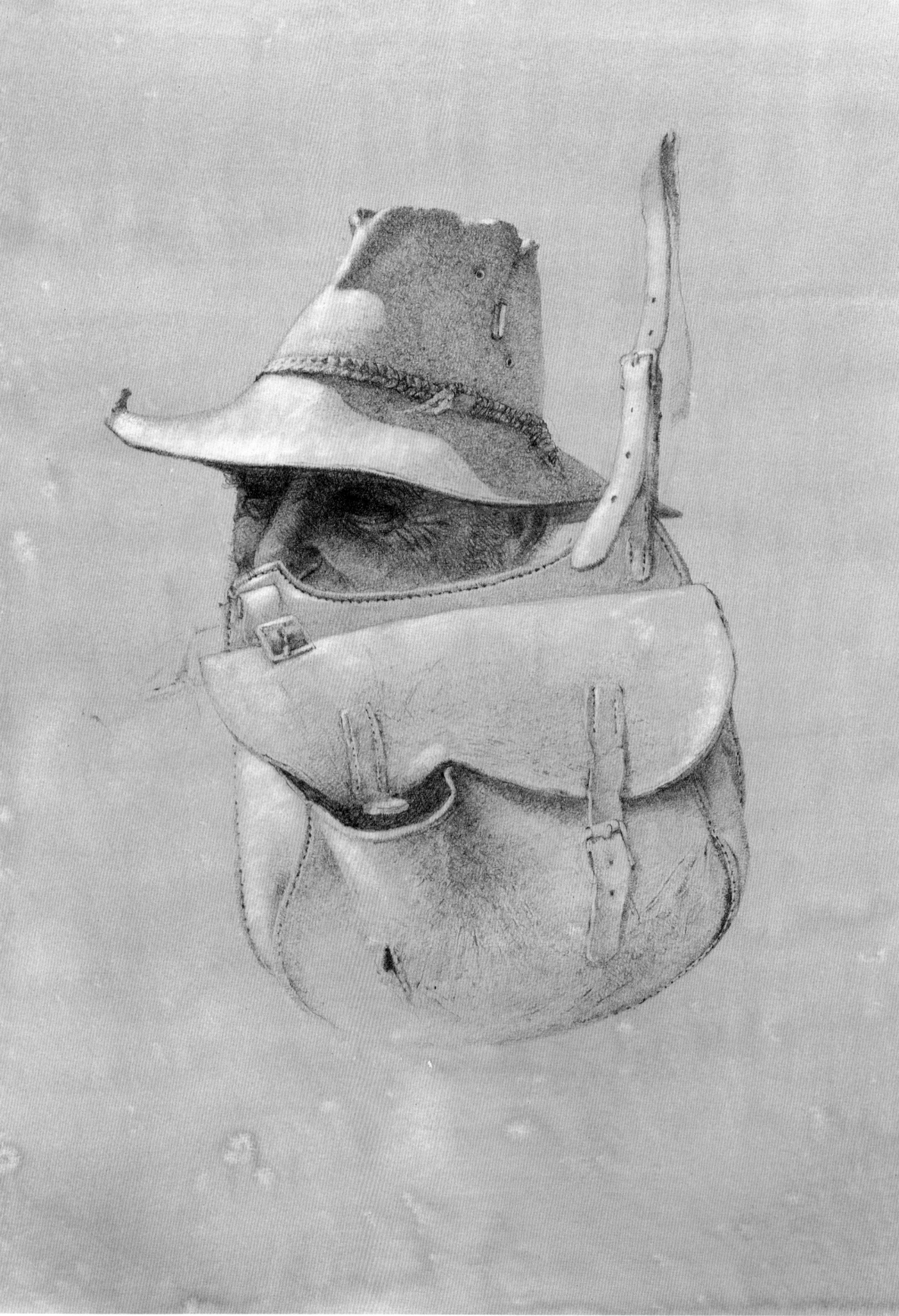

And the bush has friends to meet him,
   and their kindly voices greet him
In the murmur of the breezes
   and the river on its bars,
And he sees the vision splendid
   of the sunlit plains extended,
And at night the wondrous glory
   of the everlasting stars.

I am sitting in my dingy little office,
    where a stingy
Ray of sunlight struggles feebly
    down between the houses tall,
And the foetid air and gritty
    of the dusty, dirty city,
Through the open window floating,
    spreads its foulness over all.

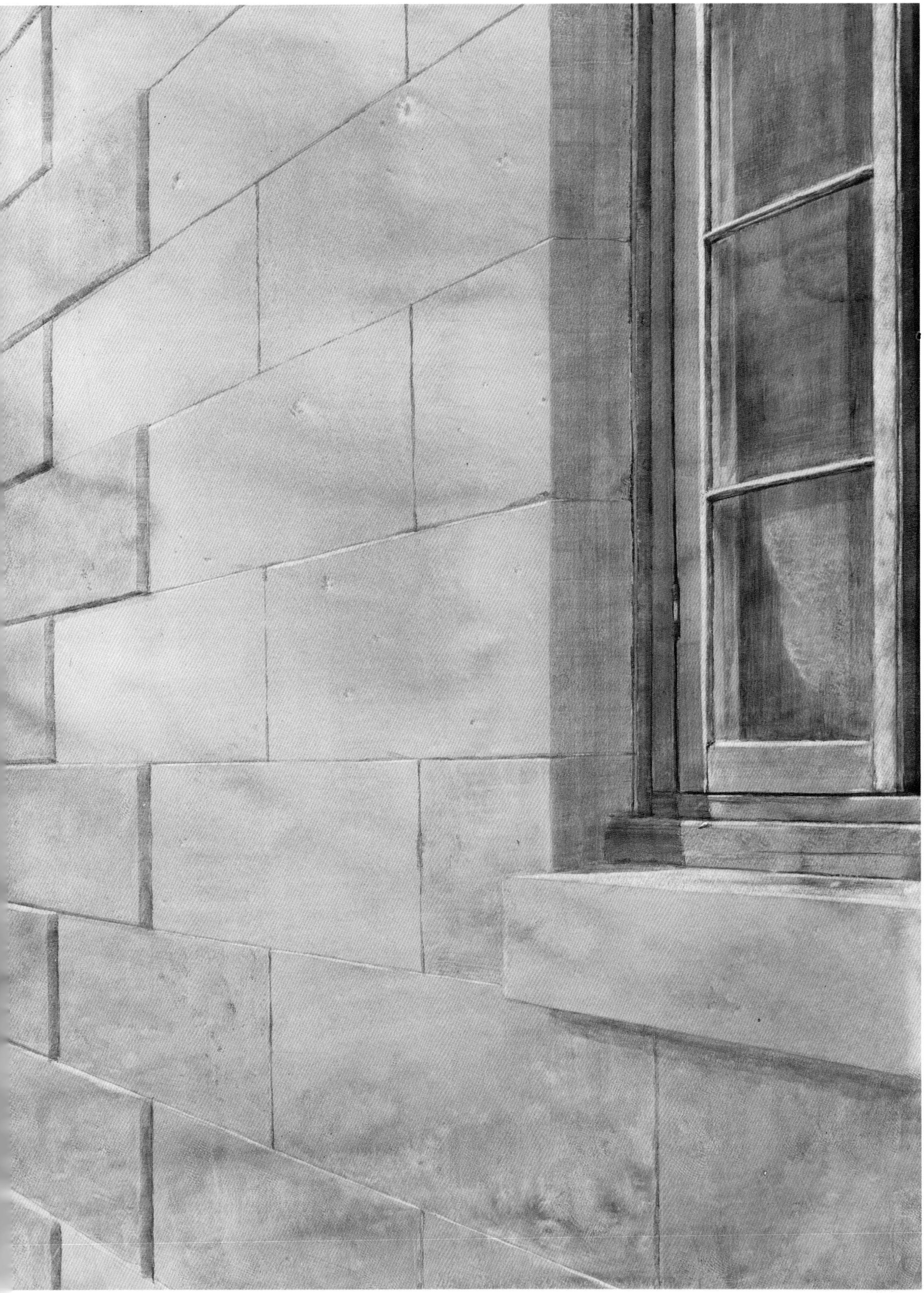

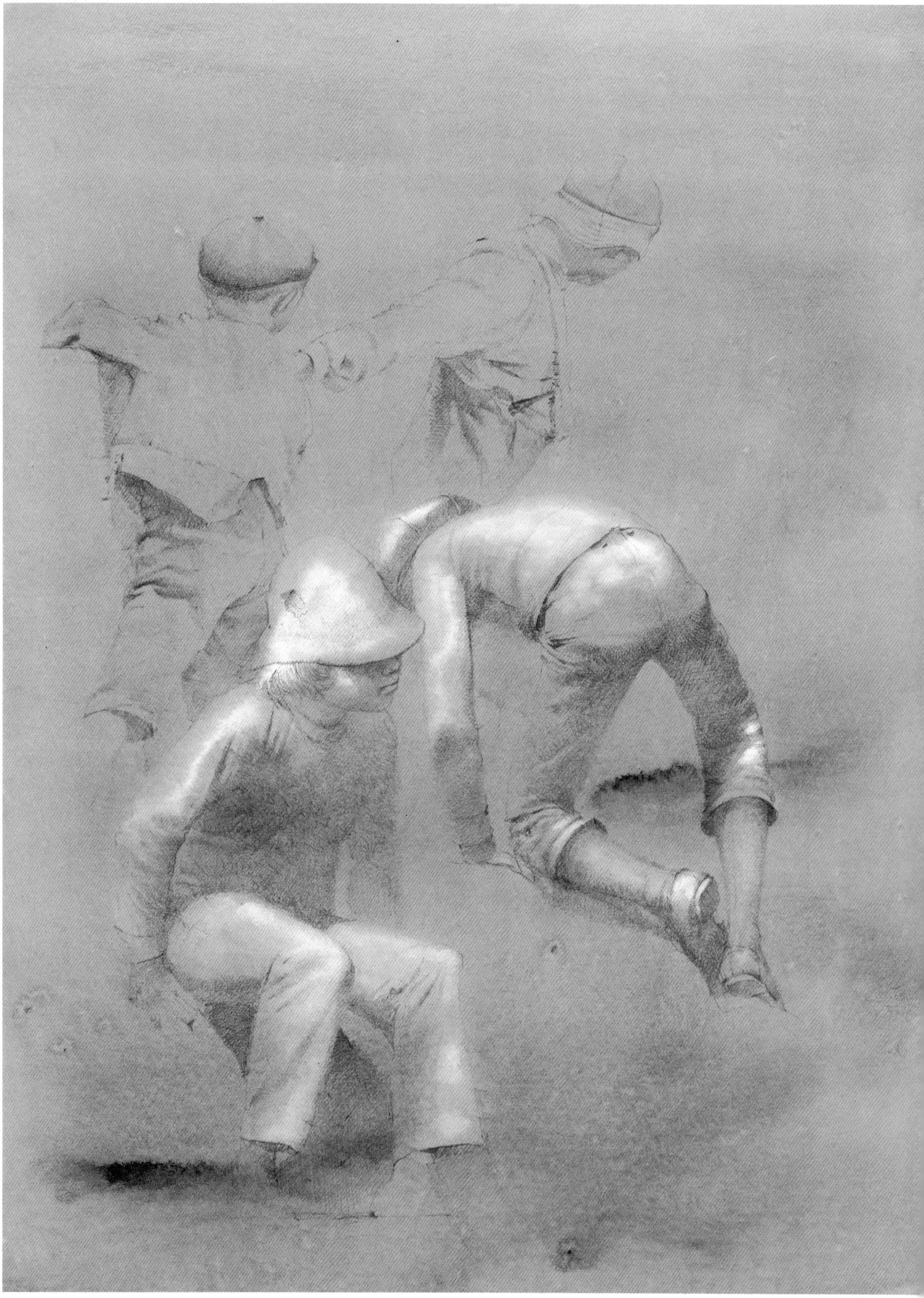

And in place of lowing cattle,
 I can hear the fiendish rattle
Of the tramways and the buses
 making hurry down the street;
And the language uninviting
 of the gutter children fighting
Comes fitfully and faintly through
 the ceaseless tramp of feet.

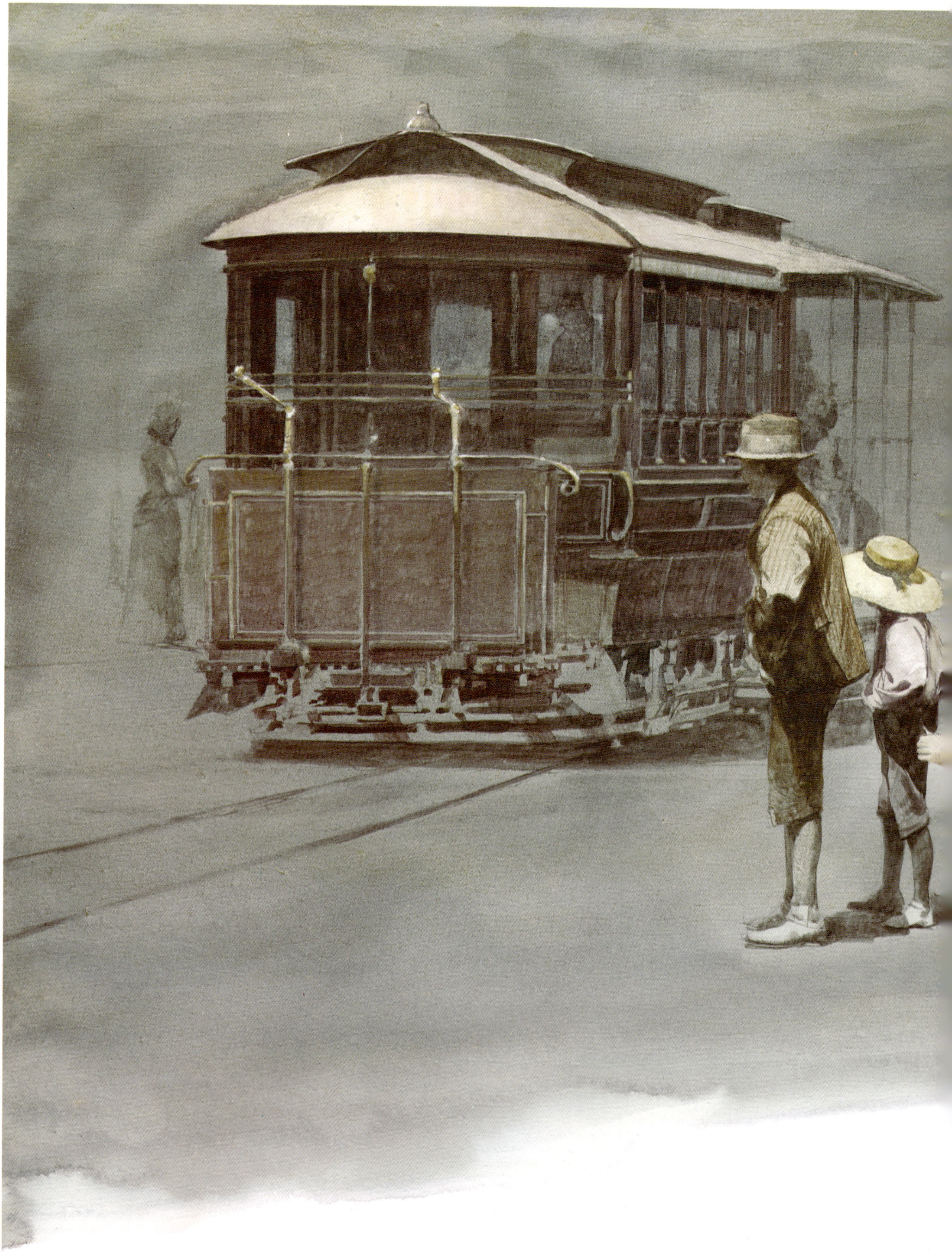

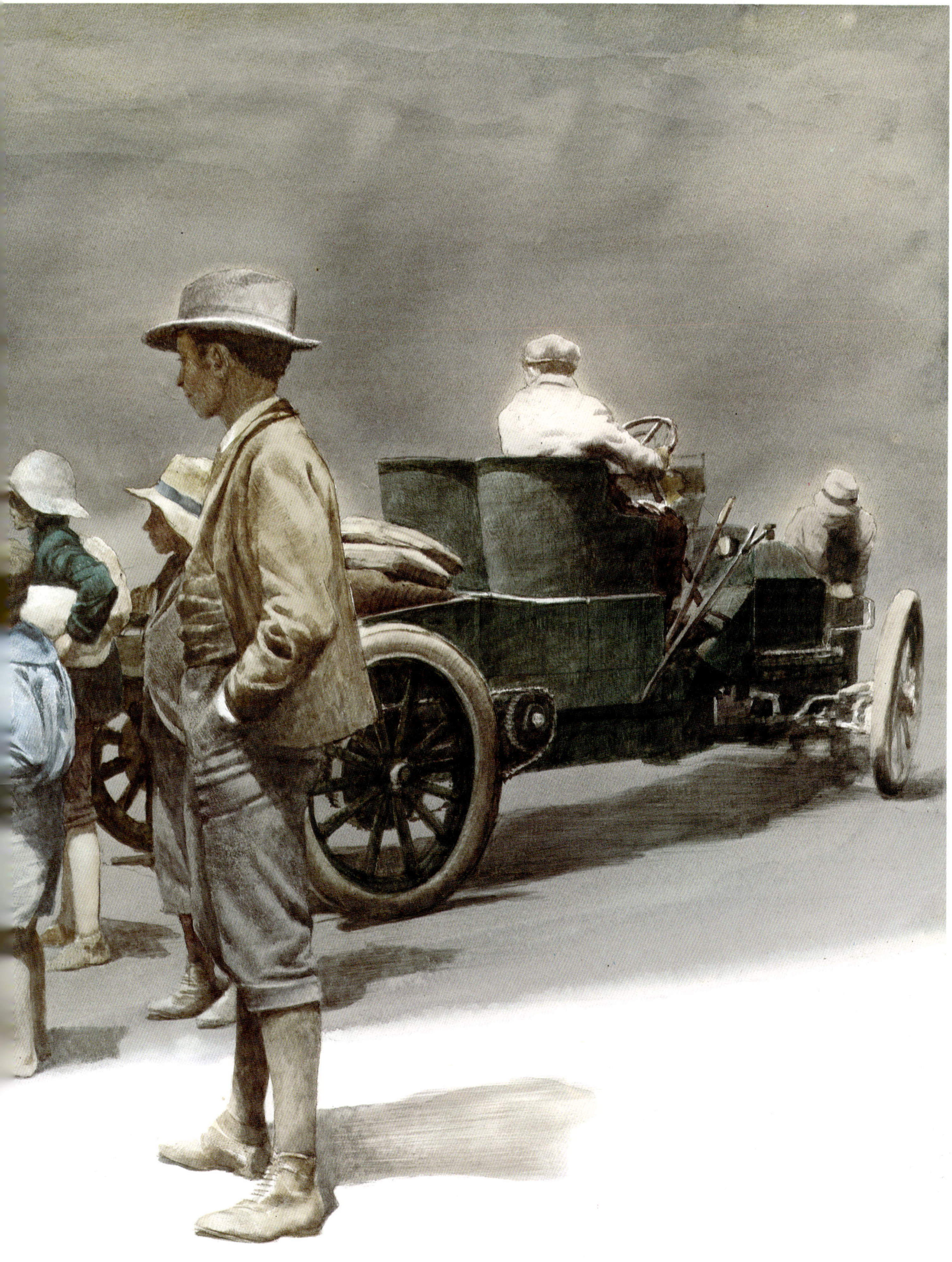

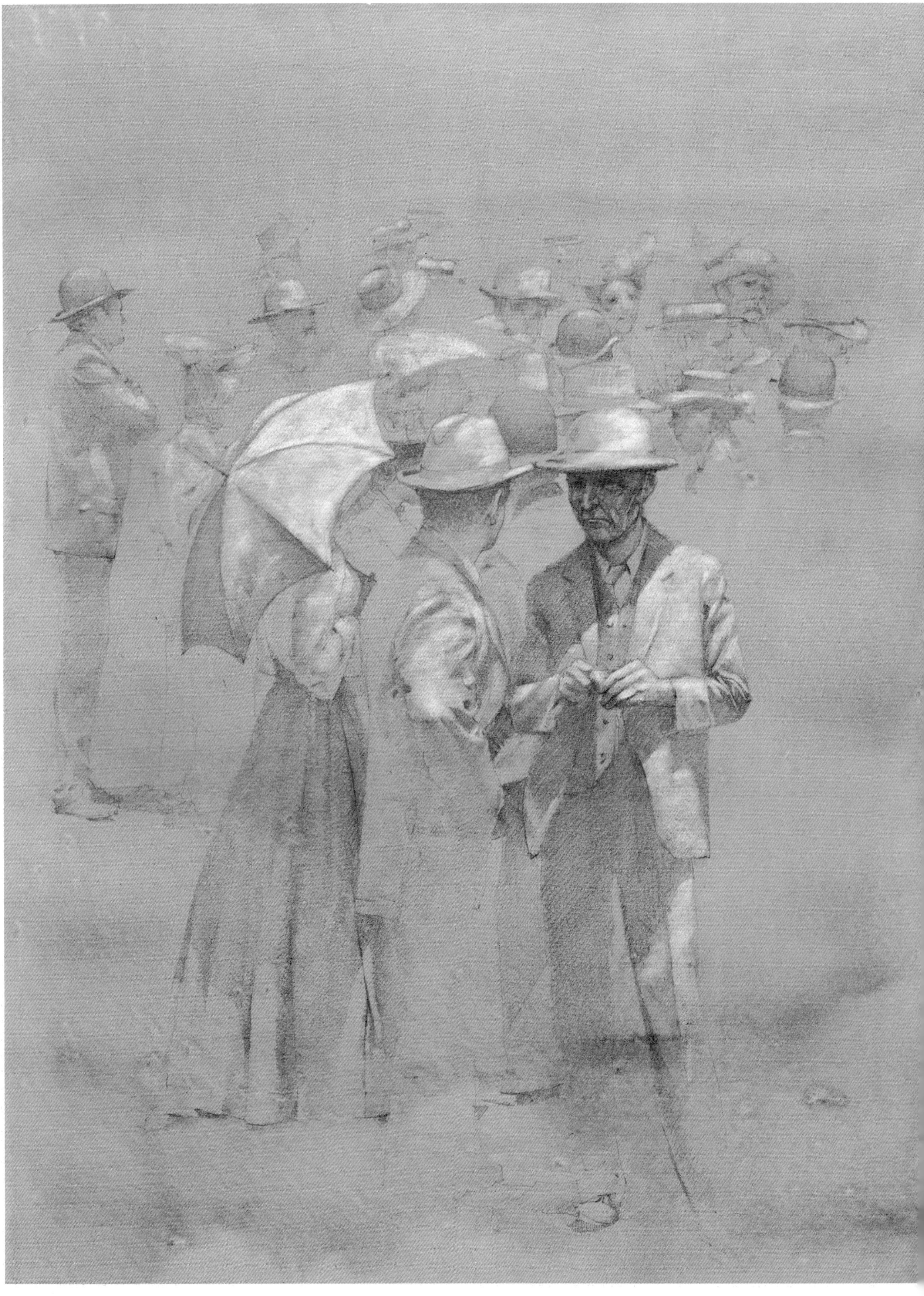

And the hurrying people daunt me,
    and their pallid faces haunt me
As they shoulder one another
    in their rush and nervous haste,
With their eager eyes and greedy,
    and their stunted forms and weedy,
For townsfolk have no time to grow,
    they have no time to waste.

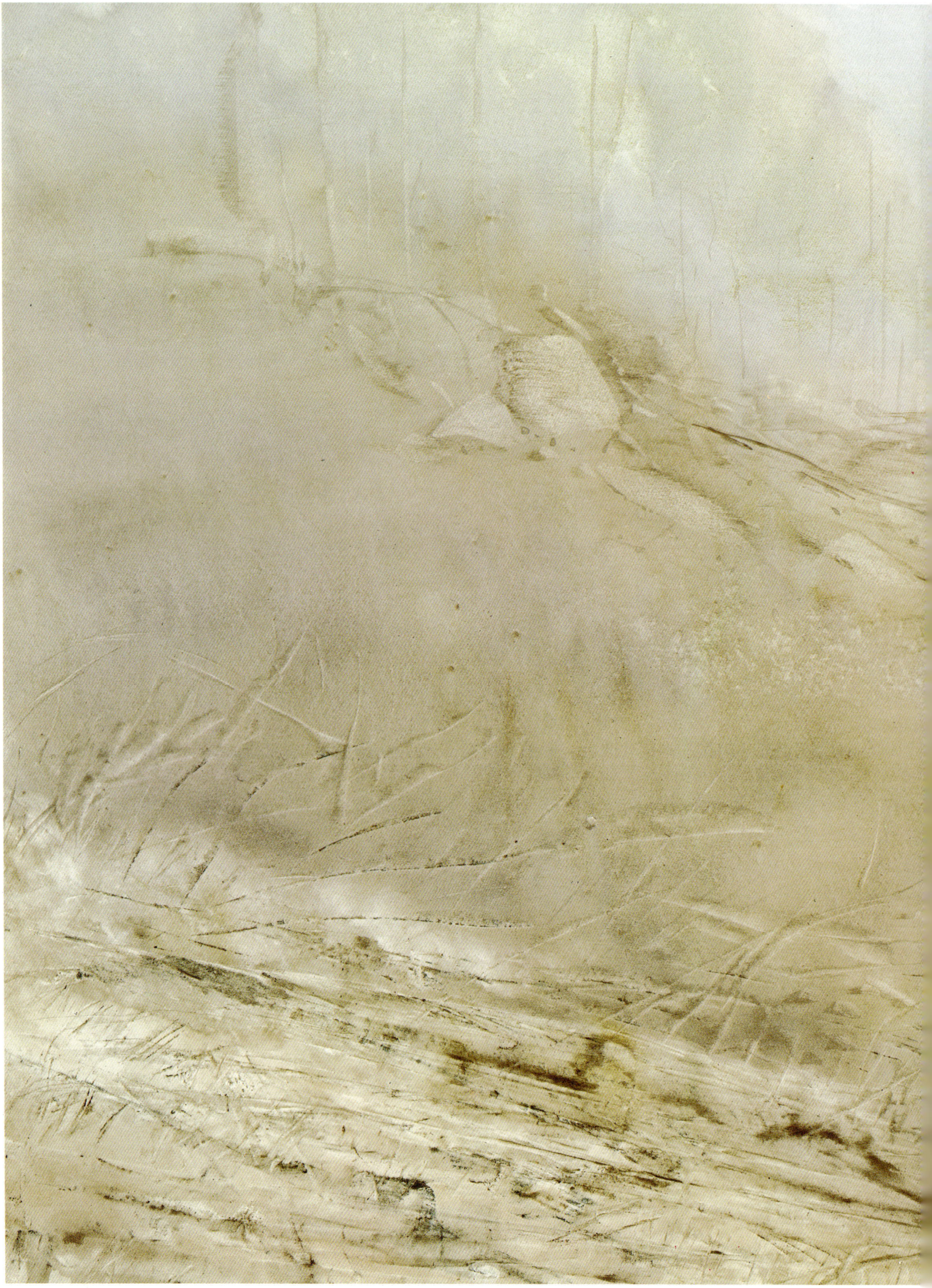

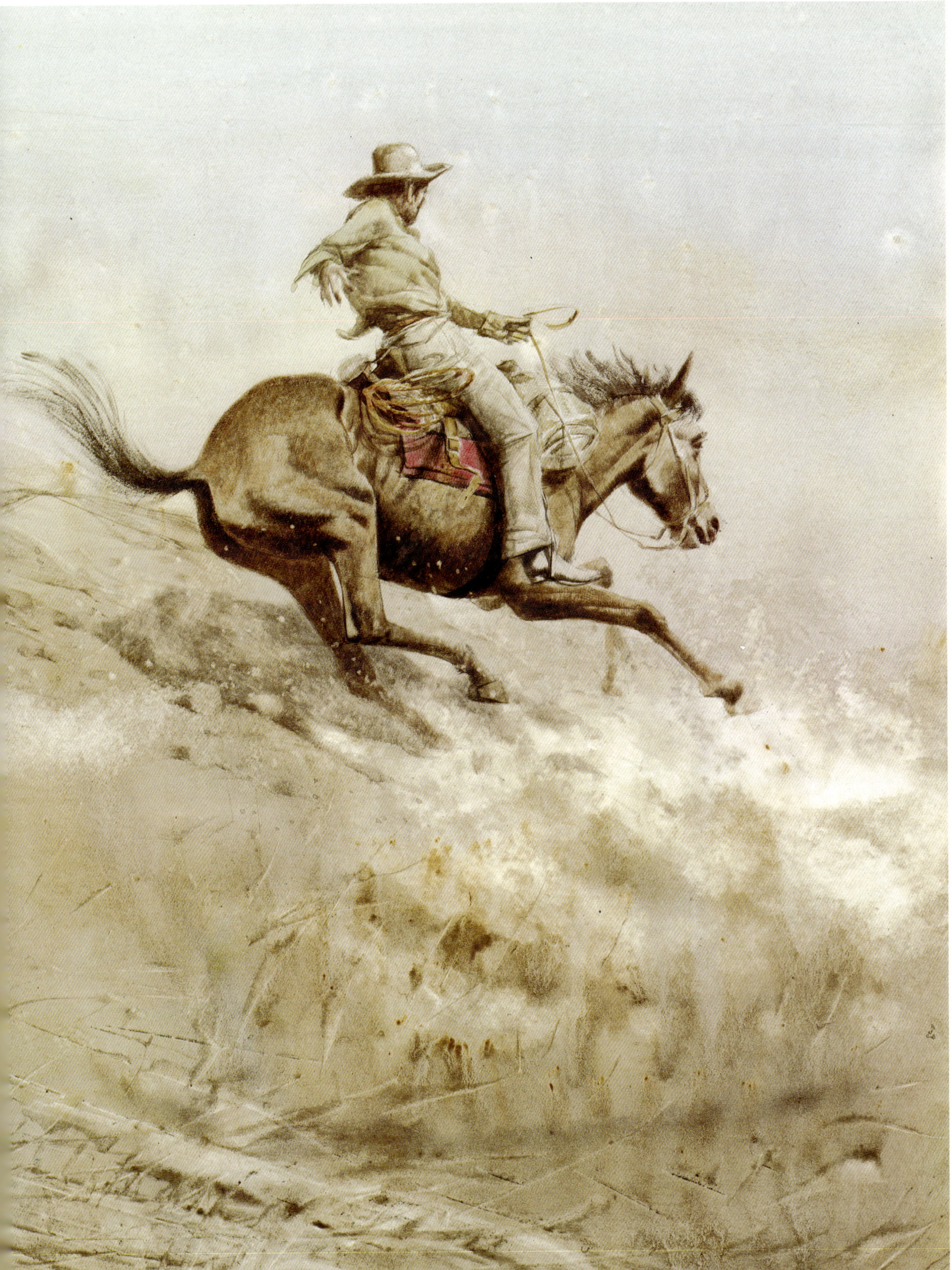

And I somehow rather fancy
    that I'd like to change with Clancy,
Like to take a turn at droving
    where the seasons come and go,
While he faced the round eternal
    of the cash-book and the journal—
But I doubt he'd suit the office,
    Clancy of The Overflow.